I F♥CK
LOVE
➤YOU

summersdale

I F*CKING LOVE YOU

An Hachette UK Company
www.hachette.co.uk

Summersdale Publishers Ltd
Part of Octopus Publishing Group Limited
Carmelite House
50 Victoria Embankment
LONDON
EC4Y 0DZ
UK

www.summersdale.com

Printed and bound in Malta

ISBN: 978-1-78685-749-1

Substantial discounts on bulk quantities of Summersdale books are available to corporations, professional associations and other organizations. For details contact general enquiries: telephone: +44 (0) 1243 771107 or email: enquiries@summersdale.com.

To ....

From ....

LET'S BE FREAKS TOGETHER.

You're my *favourite person* to drool on when I fall asleep during a *Netflix* marathon.

I couldn't live
without you...

Who'd make me
breakfast in bed?!

YOU MAY BE A DIRTY SLOTH, BUT YOU CAN STILL SHARE MY SHEETS.

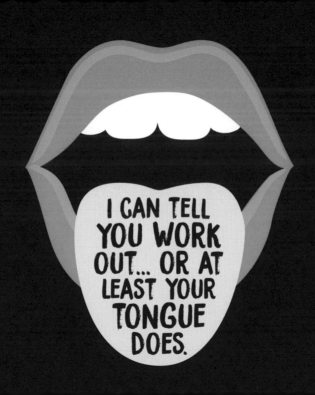

We're so lucky
to have met each
other – no one else
would have us.

Can you turn around when you're talking? I need a better view of your butt.

WERE YOU A BUNNY IN A FORMER LIFE?

BECAUSE YOU'RE ADORABLE, BUT YOUR BEDROOM IS COVERED IN PILES OF SH*T.

No matter what happens, this Christmas you're on my naughty list.

YOU'VE
BEEN RUNNING
THROUGH MY
MIND ALL DAY...
NAKED.

Your natural scent is my favourite perfume.

I LOVE MY FRIENDS, BUT THEY'RE ALL LOSERS COMPARED TO YOU.

But as soon as you
look old, this is OVER.

If there was a you-
flavoured ice cream,
I would definitely lick it.

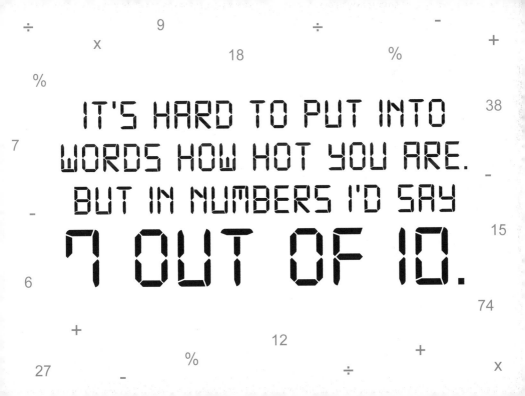

YOU'RE AN ADORABLE DWEEB.

I'm glad your ex was a dick otherwise we wouldn't be together.

WE'RE LIKE ROMEO AND JULIET...

MINUS THE FEUDING FAMILIES AND SUICIDE PACT.

CAN WE SPOON?

On a scale of hot to f*cking smokin', you're well up there.

YOU'RE THE
CAT'S
PYJAMAS.

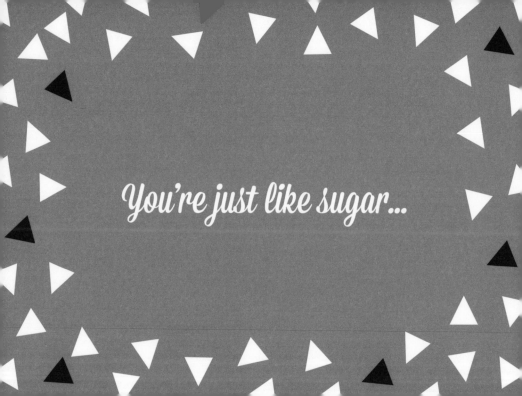

You're just like sugar...

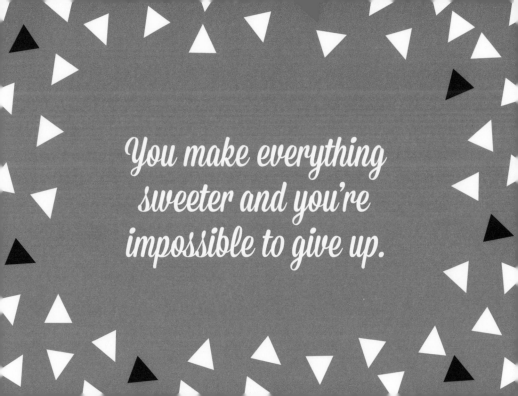

No matter what happens, I'll always be by your side... as long as that side has the best view of the TV.

I hope I don't screw this up.

We're a couple of idiots in love.

YOU MAKE
ME SO
HORNY.

SOMETIMES I WORRY YOUR GOOD LOOKS WILL FADE...

BUT THEN I GUESS SO WILL MY EYESIGHT, SO IT SHOULD ALL BE FINE.

You're abso-f*cking-lutely

turning me on right now.

YOU HAVE A WAY
WITH WORDS,
AND TONGUES.

I EVEN LOVE YOUR STINKY FARTS. WELL, MAYBE.

You're much less of a douchebag now than when we first met.

Kissing you is
totally worth it.

I KNOW I'M INTO YOU BECAUSE I WASH YOUR DIRTY UNDERWEAR.

I f*cking hate Mondays, but they're a lot better with you around.

Being with you has made me realize what a sh*tbag my ex was.

YOU'RE A DEFINITE 10...

YOU KNOW, IF THE SCALE GOES UP TO 15.

YOU ARE THE GIFT THAT KEEPS ON GIVING...

LET'S BE
F*CK-UPS
TOGETHER!

I'll show you mine if you show me yours.

WHEN I LOOK AT YOU, I WANT TO BUY THE UNIVERSE A DRINK.

Being with you is like spending every day at the fairground...

One never-ending
roller coaster.

What time is it?
Snuggle time!

YOU MAKE ME LAUGH SO HARD I WANT TO PEE.

I love you more than I love cake. And I really like cake.

IF YOU WERE THE LAST PERSON ON EARTH...

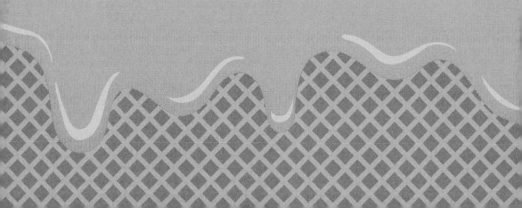

WHEN WE'RE OLD,
CAN WE STILL EAT ICE
CREAM TILL WE PUKE?

YOUR ASS IS
EVERYTHING.

I quit the gym when we met because I took up tonsil tennis instead.

IN A WORLD
FULL OF
ASSHOLES,
YOU'RE THE
BEST ONE.

You give me
butterflies...

And hickeys.

Who needs Instagram hotties when I have the real deal right here?

You're quite cute when your head's not in the gutter, literally and figuratively.

YOUR SMILE IS ALMOST AS CUTE AS YOUR ASS.

YOU MAKE MY HEART
BEAT FASTER...

I SHOULD PROBABLY SEE A DOCTOR.

THANKS FOR ALWAYS TELLING ME WHEN I'VE GOT FOOD ON MY FACE.

I WOULD WATCH YOU SLEEP, BUT THAT'S A LITTLE BIT CREEPY.

I think you're pretty...
f*cking stupid
sometimes!

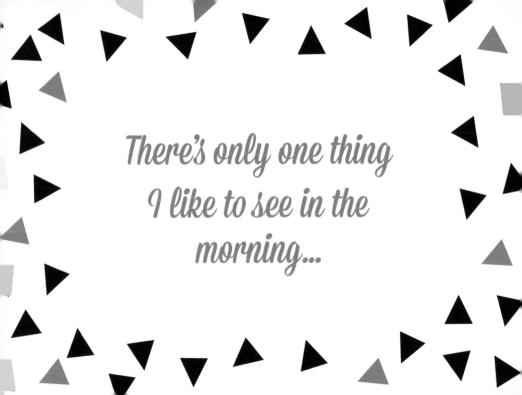

There's only one thing
I like to see in the
morning...

Your face. Oh, and a huge cup of coffee. OK, so two things.

I LOVE STEALING
ALL THE SHEETS
FROM YOU.

You're the only person I text...

when I'm on the toilet.

You look like you work out (despite the fact you're a lazy f*cker).

I never thought I'd meet someone else whose feet stink as much as mine.

I THINK...

SORRY! I LOST MY TRAIN OF THOUGHT. I WAS STARING AT YOUR BUTT.

You're like the baby koala I never had.

YOU'RE A
HOT MESS,
AND I LOVE IT.

You're the kind of
person whose puke
I wouldn't mind
cleaning up.

IF YOUR PARENTS ASK YOU, MY INTENTIONS ARE DISHONOURABLE.

I finally know how it feels to be the lights on a Christmas tree...

Because you're always turning me on.

You're everything I've ever wanted in a personal assistant.

I'M GLAD I MET YOU, BECAUSE I WAS GETTING SO SICK OF DATING.

You make the sky bluer, the grass greener, and the fridge emptier.

IT WOULD BE LIKE TASTING DOM PÉRIGNON AND THEN HAVING TO DRINK PISS.

YOU HAVE
INCREDIBLE TASTE...
IN YOUR CHOICE
OF PARTNER.

We're definitely made for each other – all our parts fit together just right.

YOU'RE THE BEST — I SH*T YOU NOT.

You remind me
of someone...

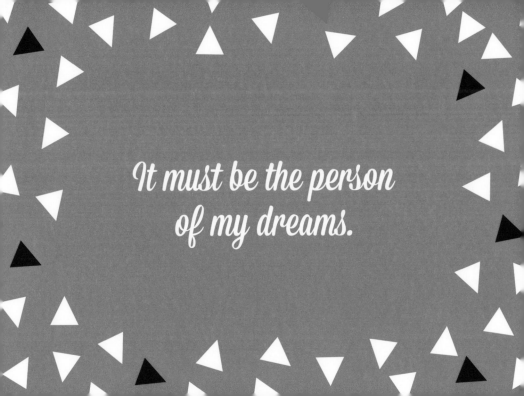

It must be the person
of my dreams.

It's so great to know that if the movie's sh*t, we can just make out instead.

I'd jump out of a plane for you. Before take-off, onto a crash mat. That's still *impressive*, right?

THANKS FOR NOT BEING ANOTHER INTERNET-DATING PSYCHO.

I LOVE YOU WITH ALL MY BUTT.

I WOULD SAY HEART, BUT MY BUTT IS BIGGER.

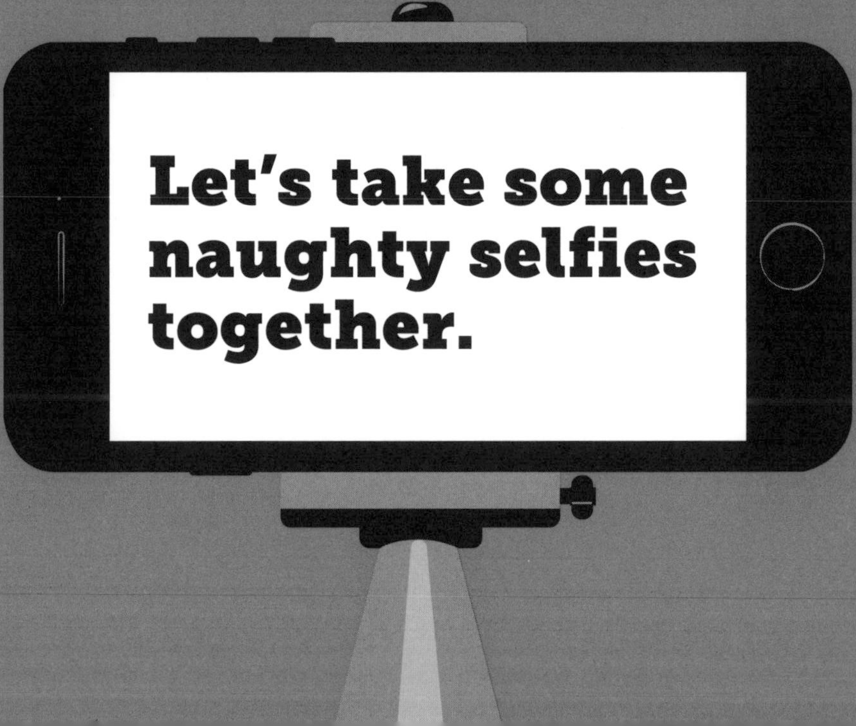
Let's take some naughty selfies together.

I LOVE YOU EVEN WHEN YOU'RE NOT NAKED.

YOU MAKE ME SWEAT, BUT IN A GOOD WAY.

Did I mention that I'm in-f*cking-fatuated with you?

You're like
chocolate...

I'M HEAD-OVER-ASS FALLING FOR YOU.

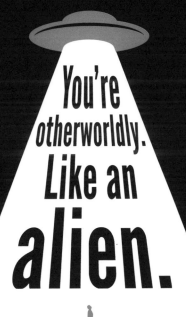

You might be an annoying prick, but at least you're my annoying prick.

I can't explain how I feel, so I'm just going to show you, with my lips.

I LOVE YOU SO MUCH MORE TODAY THAN YESTERDAY.

THAT'S BECAUSE YOU REALLY PISSED ME OFF YESTERDAY.

WHEN THE BOTTLE SPINS, I HOPE IT LANDS ON YOU.

I'd catch a grenade for you, theoretically... but when am I ever going to be in that situation?

I CAN'T BELIEVE I'M NOT F*CKING SICK OF YOU YET.

Because we always
know the right
buttons to push.

You're f*cktastic.

YOU MAKE ME STICKY IN PLACES I DIDN'T THINK WERE POSSIBLE.

Please never leave me. But if you do, could you put the bins out first?

MY HEART'S
RACING
WHENEVER
I SEE YOU...

PROBABLY BECAUSE THERE ARE SO MANY STAIRS TO GET UP TO YOUR PLACE.

YOU'RE MY
FAVOURITE PAIN
IN THE ASS.

You're almost *perfect* – any chance you come dipped in *chocolate*?

I MISS YOU
WHEN YOU'RE
NOT THERE. LIKE A
STALKER.

You make me feel
so young...

I guess you are
quite old.

Your clothes make me feel uncomfortable. Could you please take them off?

If you were an Uber,
I'd give you *five stars.*

YOU'RE SUCH A GREAT KISSER. MUST BE ALL THAT PRACTICE WE GET.

YOU'RE THE LAST THING I THINK ABOUT BEFORE I FALL ASLEEP…

BECAUSE YOU'RE
USUALLY SNORING.

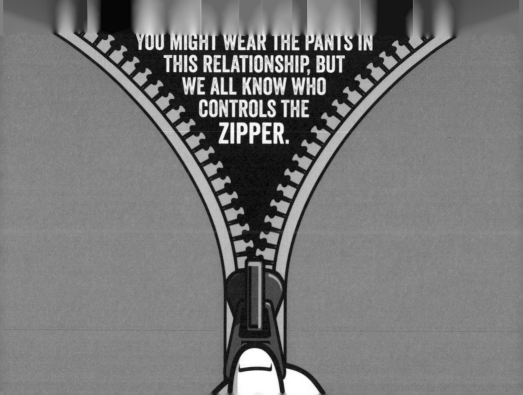

YOU MAKE ME WANT TO
BE A BETTER PERSON,
OR AT LEAST A MORE
BENDY PERSON.

KEEP CALM
AND CARRY ON
KISSING ME.

Being with you is like a fairy tale... there's always a happy ending.

You fill my heart
with joy...

And you fill my fridge with crap.

I LIKE YOU EVEN WHEN YOU DON'T REMEMBER ANYTHING I SAY.

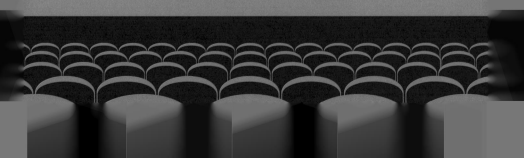

If anyone asks
what you're doing
tonight, tell them
you're all tied up.

I feel sad looking at your ass. It looks so lonely without my hands on it.

I LOVE WHEN IT'S JUST THE TWO OF US...

TO BE FAIR, WHO ELSE WOULD PUT UP WITH OUR SH*T?

I knew you
were a bad idea.
Most of my best
ideas are.